Arts & Crafts
BATIK
AND TIE-DYE

Susie O'Reilly

With photographs by Zul Mukhida

Thomson Learning
New York

Titles in this series

BATIK AND TIE-DYE
BLOCK PRINTING
MODELING
PAPERMAKING
STENCILING
WEAVING

Frontispiece *A piece of tie-dyed cotton from Sierra Leone, West Africa.*

First published in the
United States in 1993 by
Thomson Learning
115 Fifth Avenue
New York, NY 10003

First published in 1993 by
Wayland (Publishers) Ltd

Cataloging-in-Publication Data
applied for

ISBN: 1-56847-064-9

Printed in Italy.

CONTENTS

Words printed in **bold** appear in the glossary.

GETTING STARTED

When artists look at blank canvas, they imagine vivid paintings. Some
people feel the same way when they see plain **fabric**. They picture it alive
with color and movement. Long ago, people got the idea of making
patterns in fabric by protecting some parts from **dye** and letting other parts
soak up all the glorious color. This is called **resist** dyeing. Two popular
methods are batik and tie-dye.

These designs ▶
*were inspired by
the artist's
knowledge of
traditional batik.*

▼ *People in Africa
wear clothes made
from tie-dyed and
batik fabrics.*

In tie-dye, the fabric is folded, tied, or
stitched. In batik, melted wax, flour paste,
rice **starch**, clay—or whatever is most
easily available—is applied to the fabric.
Both methods protect parts of the fabric
from being colored by dye.

People around the world who have a
tradition of making resist-dyed fabrics
value them highly. They are worn by rich
and important people and at special
events such as weddings and funerals.

People from many developing countries
still make and wear resist-dyed **textiles**.
They use methods handed down over the
years through their families. Artists,
craftspeople, and **designers** from other
parts of the world use these traditional
techniques as an exciting source of ideas
for their own work.

This book will help you to explore some
of the many possibilities of batik and tie-
dye.

◀ *Here are some ideas for things you can make: a patchwork quilt, a pillow, or a picture.*

Safety
■ Always make sure you have a fire extinguisher or bucket of sand nearby in case of fire.
■ Make sure your hair is tied back and sleeves rolled up when using heating equipment.

SETTING UP YOUR WORK AREA

You will need to gather these tools and materials to get started:

Fabric
Cut white or beige fabric into squares (10 to 12 inches) or rectangles (6 by 12 inches). Cotton, silk, and other natural fabrics work well. Avoid artificial fibers, such as polyester and wash-and-wear fabric.

General equipment
Old newspapers (to protect work surfaces and floors)
Apron, rubber gloves

Drying rack or line
Plastic bowls or dishpans
Cold-water dyes (see page 18)
Salt
Wooden spoons
Iron
Needles, pins, thread
Scissors
Paper and pencils

For batik
Wooden frame or cardboard box for stretching fabric
Electric or gas stove ring
Old saucepan and tin can

Batik wax (from an arts and crafts store) or paraffin wax (from a hardware store)
Household candles
Wax crayons
Egg poacher or muffin tin
Paint brushes
Old screwdrivers, knives, forks to scrape off wax
Tacks or staples
Food coloring

For tie-dye
String
Pebbles or dried peas
Bulldog clips
Plastic wrap

BATIK AROUND THE WORLD

It is not known exactly when or where people started making batik-patterned cloths. **Archaeologists** have found evidence of batik in the Far East, the Middle East, Central Asia, and India. They have uncovered scraps of ancient batik cloth, and paintings and sculptures showing people wearing what seem to be batik fabrics. Batik is still made all over the world. Some methods result in big, bold, powerful designs. Others give delicate, finely detailed patterns.

In Indonesia, batiks have fine, delicate lines and carefully placed dots. The wax is skillfully dribbled onto the cloth using a special tool, called a *tjanting*, which gives crisp, controlled patterns.

▲ *Delicately patterned cloth from Bali, Indonesia.*

◄ *An Indonesian craftsperson using a* tjanting.

Some Indonesian batik-makers choose to use **brittle** waxes that crack and allow the dye to seep into the cloth. Others prefer to use a more **flexible** wax, which does not crack as it hardens, and so resists the dye completely.

In Japan, rice paste and paste made from rice starch are the most widely available resists. The Japanese have developed a number of techniques for decorating the silks and cottons used to make screens, cloths, and **kimonos**. On Okinawa, one of Japan's islands, a very special technique called *bingata* was developed. Rice paste was **stenciled** onto the cloth to make delicate patterns of flowers, birds, and trees.

In parts of China, people made blue and white patterns on coarse cloth using a bean curd resist. The resist dried in the sun and could be rubbed off easily.

The people of the Ivory Coast in West Africa smear cloth with a paste made from rice starch. They use a comb to scrape patterns into the wet paste.

▲ *The craftspeople of Nigeria in Africa make big, bold patterns using flour paste to resist the dye.*

▼ *This fabric from India has been prepared with paste and is ready to go into the dye bath.*

▼ *These colorful batik fabrics will be made into turbans and dresses.*

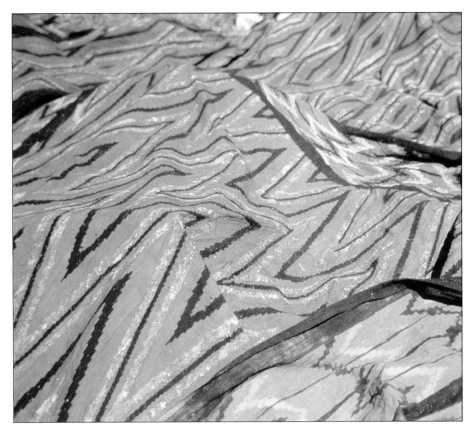

STEP-BY-STEP BATIK

Dye your own picture or pattern into cloth using batik. Cover the whole area with wax and scrape it away from the parts where you want color, or put wax only on the parts you want to keep white. Design your picture on a piece of paper, cover your work surface with newspaper, and follow these instructions.

TURN TO PAGES 22–25 FOR IDEAS ABOUT USING YOUR BATIK.

1 Wet a piece of cloth. Tack or staple it onto a wooden frame or shallow cardboard box with the bottom cut out. The cloth will shrink as it dries, giving a tight surface.

4 Scratch a pattern or picture into the wax with a fork, darning needle, screwdriver, or other tool. Turn the frame or box over. Scrape away the wax in all of the same places that you scraped it on the front of the cloth. Remember, the dye will color the areas where you scraped off the wax.

2 Put some batik wax or paraffin in a tin can and stand the can in a saucepan of water. Make sure the water does not come more than halfway up the side of the can. Put the pan over low heat on a ring, so the wax melts. **Ask an adult to help you do this.**

3 Using a stiff-haired brush, such as a household paint brush, paint the melted wax onto the cloth. Coat both sides. Let it dry.

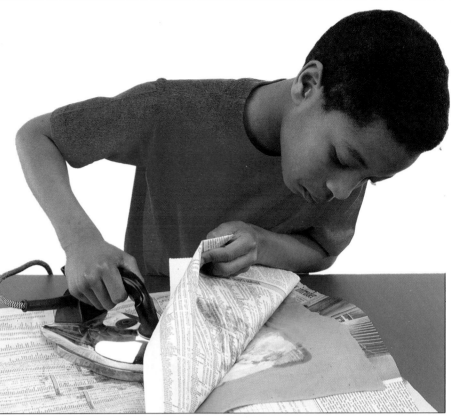

5 Now dye the cloth. Turn to pages 18–19 for information about how to do this.

6 When the cloth is dyed and dry, remove the wax. Scrape off as much as you can with a table knife.

7 Put the cloth between layers of newspaper. Press a warm iron over the top of the paper. The heat will melt the wax and the newspaper will soak it up. To get all the wax out you will have to change the layers of newspaper several times. **Ask an adult to help you use the iron.**

8 Wash the cloth several times in warm, soapy water. Rinse well, dry, and give the cloth a good iron.

MORE BATIK IDEAS

USING WAX CRAYONS

1 Find an old egg poacher or muffin tin. Put small pieces of wax crayons in each holder. Keep colors separate.

2 Half-fill the pan with water and put it over low heat on the ring. **Always ask an adult to help you do this. Be careful not to let the pan boil dry.**

3 Using stiff-haired brushes, one for each color, paint the melted

wax onto the fabric. If it is hot, it will stain the fabric the color of the crayons.

4 Brush a cold-water dye of a different color all over the fabric. It will fill in the background.

5 Iron off the wax between layers of newspaper. Wash the cloth in soapy water, rinse, and iron.

USING CANDLES

1 Prepare a fabric frame or use a box (see page 8).

2 Light an ordinary household candle (freezing it for a few hours beforehand helps it burn evenly). Drip wax over your fabric. Experiment with trailing small dots in stripes or spirals. **Ask an adult to help you. Make sure you blow the candle out afterward.**

3 Dye the cloth following the instructions on pages 18–19. Iron off the wax between layers of newspaper.

DECORATING EGGS

1 Hard boil some eggs in a pan of water or poke small holes in both ends of a raw egg and blow it out.

2 Paint patterns on the eggs using a brush dipped in melted wax. You can use wax crayons or candle wax.

3 Put the eggs in a bowl of water colored with food dye.

Dye your eggs in a bowl of ▶ *water and food dye. Decorated eggs in a basket look pretty at Easter time.*

TIE-DYE AROUND THE WORLD

Tie-dye is practiced today all over the world. In many regions,
people have been using the same techniques for hundreds of years.
They still use very simple, basic equipment.

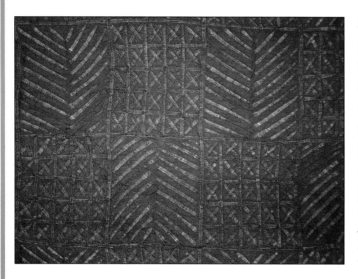

Many West African people continue to produce tie-dyed fabrics, some for everyday wear, some for special occasions. The Yoruba people of Nigeria use a combination of tying, pleating, and sewing. They also sew or tie objects they have found into the cloth to create unusual patterns. Using **indigo** dye, they produce wonderful, dark blue patterns in cotton cloth. The women do the tying and the dyeing. The men **finish** the cloth by beating it until it shines.

▲ *The patterns on this Nigerian cloth were made by sewing in raffia threads to resist the dye.*

Tie-dyed fabric from Japan. Large patterns ▶ *are built up by repeating simple motifs.*

▼ *Tie-dyed fabric drying in the sun in Nigeria. Craftspeople often work outdoors.*

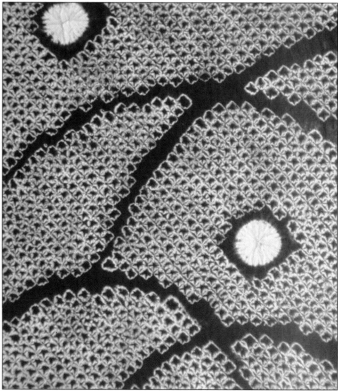

In India, tie-dyed fabrics called *bandhani* are made and worn in the states of Gujarat and Rajasthan. *Bandhani* are made of fine silk that is folded, dampened, and pressed over a board of pins. The pins may be arranged in many different ways, and each pattern has a particular meaning. The women and children grow their nails or use a special metal thimble to pick up the tiny points of fabric off the pins. They tie the points with cotton thread.

Japanese tie-dye uses delicate colors and elaborate patterns. Large patterns are built up by repeating simple **motifs**. After the knots are untied, the fabric often remains dimpled. This makes it soft and stretchy. Clothes made from this fabric are very comfortable.

▲ Bandhani *from India are comfortable to wear. Dimples left by the knots have lots of "give."*

▼ *In Japan, tie-dyed fabric is called* shibori, *meaning tied or knotted. This piece has been untied after it was dyed.*

STEP-BY-STEP TIE-DYE

Cut plain cotton fabric into several 10-inch squares. Experiment with different ways of tying up the squares. Each way will give you a different pattern when the fabric is dyed. With practice, you'll learn how to achieve certain results—but you can never predict exactly what will happen!

2 Tie in the pea or pebble by tightly wrapping some string around the cloth. Fasten it with a knot. The tighter the binding, the more the fabric will resist the dye.

3 Dye and rinse the fabric. Turn to pages 18–19 for information on how to do this.

1 Lay the cloth flat. Place a dried pea or pebble in the center.

4 When the fabric is dry, untie the string and iron the cloth.

VARIATIONS

1 Roll the fabric up and tie it at intervals.

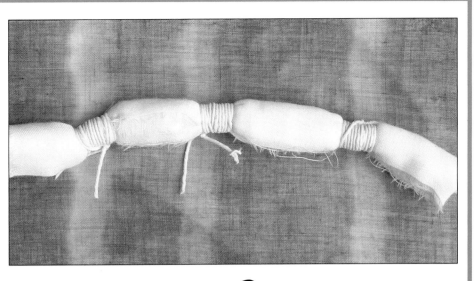

2 Place a pebble in the center of a piece of cloth. Place smaller pebbles in a pattern over the rest of the cloth. Mark their positions with a soft pencil. Tie the pebbles into the cloth at each mark.

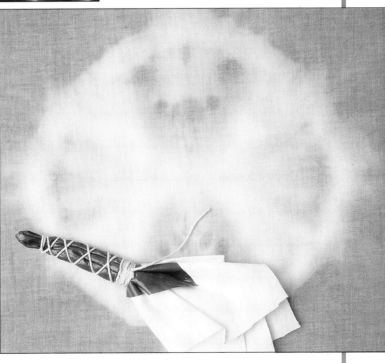

3 Tie a piece of plastic wrap around the area you want to protect from dyeing.

There are many more ways that you can tie the fabric. Poke a few small holes in the plastic wrap for interesting effects.

MORE TIE-DYE IDEAS

There are many ways you can prevent dye from getting to areas of your fabric. Try using clamps or sewing with a needle and thread. Here are some ideas to get you started.

TURN TO PAGES 22–25 FOR IDEAS ABOUT USING YOUR TIE-DIE.

1 Place a saucer in the middle of your cloth. Trace the saucer with a soft pencil.

2 With a needle and thread, sew tacking stitches into the cloth, following the pencil line. Make two more circles of tacking stitches.

3 Tie a pebble into the center of the cloth. Pull the threads to gather the cloth up tightly, so that the folds resist the dye. This technique, using sewing, is called *tritik*.

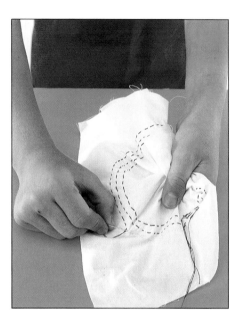

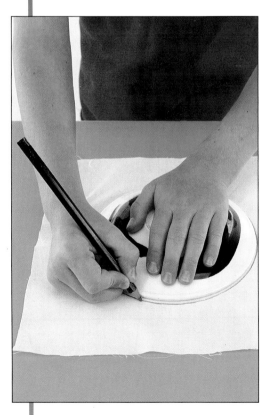

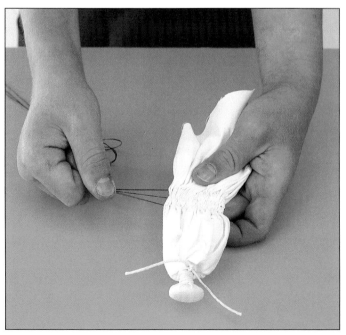

4 Turn to pages 18–19 for instructions on dyeing and rinsing.

Other Ideas

1 Fold the cloth in four, then bind it with string.

2 Fold the cloth like an accordian. Iron in the pleats and clamp the cloth top and bottom using bulldog clips.

Using Dyes

You can buy dyes that are ready to use straight from the package. Deka, Procion, and Jacquard are brands of cold-water dyes. You can buy them at most arts and crafts stores. They are easy to use and will not melt the wax on your batiks. Different dyes are prepared in different ways. Always follow the instructions on the package and cover your work surface with newspaper. Here are some guidelines.

1 Put on rubber gloves and an apron. Dyes stain nearly everything they come in contact with.

2 Mix the dye powder with some hot water. **Ask an adult to help you do this**.

3 Add a tablespoon of salt. Salt helps the cloth

soak up the dye. You may also want to add special cold-dye fixer.

4 Put the dye in a large plastic bowl or tray. Add cold water. Stir very thoroughly with a wooden spoon or disposable paint stirrer.

5 Dampen the fabric before you put it in the dye bowl. This helps the dye to soak into the fibers.

6 Leave the fabric in the dye bowl for one hour. Stir gently every now and then to make sure the dye colors the fabric evenly.

7 Take the fabric out of the dye. Rinse it really well in the sink, changing the water three or four times to get rid of the extra dye.

8 Hang the dyed cloth up to dry. Then remove the wax or string resist. With tie-dye you can remove the string when the cloth is wet, but the dye might run.

9 You can also paint dye onto your cloth with a brush. This works well if you are making a batik on a frame or cardboard box.

10 If you are working on a piece that uses several colors, you will want to dye the cloth more than once. Turn to pages 20–21 for advice on this.

▼ *The soft brown color of this fabric comes from onion skins.*

NATURAL DYES

In the past, people around the world developed dyes from parts of plants, animals, rocks, and earth. These are still used today.

You can make your own dyes, too. Onion skins give soft brown, orange, and yellow colors. Boil the skins in a saucepan of water for twenty minutes. Put your cloth in the pan and leave for one hour. Rinse and dry. Try boiling beets, blueberries, or plant stems. You will need to experiment to get the range of colors you need.

PLANNING COLOR

There are three pairs of **primary colors**—two yellows, two reds, and two blues. These are: lemon yellow and chrome yellow; crimson red and vermilion red; Prussian blue and ultramarine blue. By mixing these colors and adding black in different amounts, you can make all the other colors. For example, chrome yellow and vermilion red make orange. Lemon yellow and ultramarine blue make bright green.

You can make your own colors by mixing dye powders or liquids before you put the fabric into the dye bath. You can also make colors by dyeing the cloth in a series of different dye baths. This is how you make white, yellow, and green patterning.

1 Attach your cloth to a frame. Wax the area you want to keep white. Paint yellow dye over the cloth and let it dry.

2 Now wax the yellow areas that you want to keep yellow.

Remember that different fibers will take the same dye quite differently.

Also, plan carefully which colors to place next to each other. Experiment using squares of colored paper, cut out and used in different ways.

▼ *Putting different colors next to each other produces various effects. Experiment using colored-paper shapes.*

3 Paint blue or turquoise dye over the cloth and let it dry. Take the cloth off the frame and iron off the wax. The areas of the fabric that were dyed yellow and then blue will be green.

It is very important to plan the order in which you use the colored dyes. Some colors are weak and will not show up over stronger colors. The correct order is lemon yellow (which is the weakest color), followed by chrome yellow, vermilion, crimson, ultramarine, Prussian blue, and black.

PROJECTS

People all over the world use batik and tie-dye to make fabric for special clothes and other objects. There are lots of things that you can make, too.

DYEING A T-SHIRT

1 You need a plain white or light-colored T-shirt or vest. Read the label to make sure it is made of cotton. Cotton takes color well from cold-water dyes and will produce the best results.

2 If you are using a new T-shirt, wash it to get rid of the finish. The finish prevents the fabric from taking the dye.

3 Plan your batik or tie-dye design. Look at the chapters in this book to plan which technique to use, how to get the colors you want, and the number of dye baths you will need. Make some sketches of possible designs.

▲ *Plan a design around the neck and sleeves only, or in bands across the top and bottom of the T-shirt.*

4 Here are some ideas. You could make a T-shirt with the design just on the front, on the sleeves, or all over.

Remember: your T-shirt must be washed separately from other clothes. Some of the dye may run in the wash and stain other clothes.

Make a wide border around ▶ *the neckline and scatter smaller patterns over the body of the T-shirt.*

Cover the front, back, and ▶ *sleeves with small circles.*

▼ *Make a big circular pattern to cover the front.*

MORE PROJECTS

You can batik or tie-dye inexpensive cotton handkerchiefs, socks, T-shirts, and other items from a discount store or thrift shop. But you might decide it's more fun to start from scratch. If you plan to turn your own piece of batik or tie-dye into something useful, you'll need to make sure the edges of the fabric don't **fray** by sewing a hem.

MAKING A HANDKERCHIEF, NAPKIN, OR SCARF

1 Turn the fabric over so the wrong side faces up.

2 Turn over a half-inch of fabric along one edge. Iron it flat so that it stays turned over.

3 Turn over another half-inch. Now the cut edge of the fabric is hidden in the fold. Iron or pin the fold.

4 Thread a needle with fine sewing cotton, using a color that matches the background color of your fabric.

5 Sew the hem with tiny stitches, as invisible as you can. Make a stich every quarter or half-inch.

6 Do the same on all four sides of the cloth.

MAKING A WALL HANGING

1 Think about where you are going to display your wall hanging and decide what size it will be. Also decide what colors look good. Design and dye your piece of fabric.

2 Hem the sides only, following the instructions opposite.

5 Now make a hanging rope. Cut a piece of thin string about ten times the length of one of your dowels. Dip it in one of the dye baths you used for your hanging and let it dry.

6 Fold the string in half, half again, half again, and half again. Bind it at intervals. Dye it in another dye bath you used for your hanging.

7 When it is dry, cut the string into three equal parts and braid it. Attach the braid to the top rod and hang on the wall.

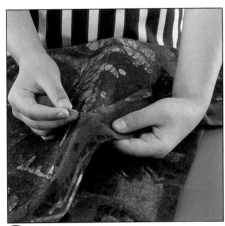

3 To hang the piece, you will need two **dowels** slightly wider than your wall hanging, to go at the top and bottom. **Ask an adult to cut the dowels to the correct length**.

4 Make hems to hold the dowels. To do this start a hem as before but make the second turn two inches deep, rather than a half-inch. Insert the dowels.

THE GALLERY

Look at the pictures on these pages. They have been chosen to give you ideas and inspiration for your batik and tie-dye designs.

▼ *Straight and curvy tree trunks.*

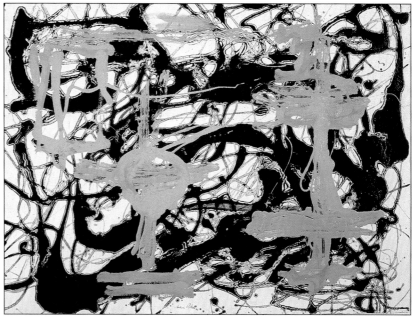

▲ *A painting by Jackson Pollock.*

Start your own collection of shapes, colors, and patterns that you really enjoy looking at. Collect shells and pebbles, candy wrappers, pieces of driftwood, or scraps of broken china. Use paper and crayons to make rubbings of natural objects, such as tree bark, or manufactured items, such as manhole covers. Cut out pictures from magazines, buy postcards, and take photographs.

Display your collection on a bulletin board. Start making a scrapbook and find a shelf or window sill where you can display your objects.

Broken tiles.

◀ *Giraffe markings.*

▲ *Pine cones.*

◀ *Parasols.*

A peacock feather. ▶

▼ *Sand patterns.*

DEVELOPING DESIGN IDEAS

Use your collection of pictures, scraps, and objects to develop design ideas. One item can suggest many different ideas. For instance, choose a three-dimensional object (something that has height, width, and depth), such as this shell. The shell has shape, pattern, and color, but you do not need to use all of this in your design. Instead, select some aspects of the shell and develop them.

1 Look at the shell from a number of different angles and make some quick drawings to record what you see.

2 Looking down on the top of the shell might make you think of tie-dyeing a piece of fabric by rolling it up and tying it at intervals.

3 From the side the shell has a very simple shape. It looks a bit like a brush mark. Try to copy the shape on a sheet of paper using a stiff brush dipped in hot wax. Try making patterns by arranging the shapes in different ways. Brush over the paper with colored ink. The wax will resist the ink and show you how the design might look on fabric.

4 Look at the pattern on the shell's surface. Hold the shell in one hand and draw the part of the pattern you can see. Turn the shell around and draw the part of the pattern you can see then. Keep doing this until you have drawn the pattern all the way around. Use the entire pattern for your design, or choose part of it to enlarge.

5 Look at the colors of the shell. You might decide to dye your fabric the same colors. Or you might decide to choose other colors for your work.

GLOSSARY

Archaeologists People who find out what happened in the past by studying ancient remains.

Brittle Easily cracked.

Designers People who create the shape and style of an object or decoration. Their ideas are used in making the finished product.

Dowels Thin wooden rods.

Dye A liquid used to color fabric or other materials.

Fabric Cloth.

Flexible Able to bend without breaking or cracking.

Finish To put a special surface on a piece of cloth, to change the way it looks, feels, or behaves.

Fray To wear away or come undone at the edges.

Indigo A natural dye that comes from a plant. It gives a rich purple-blue color.

Kimonos Long, loose robes worn in Japan.

Motifs Shapes that are repeated to make a pattern.

Primary colors The colors red, blue, and yellow, from which all other colors can be made.

Resist Any kind of coating that is used to keep dye from getting to certain parts of a piece of cloth.

Starch A kind of sticky sugar found in many plants, particularly rice and other cereals.

Stenciled Applied using a stencil. This is a sheet of stiff paper or plastic with holes cut in the shape of a design. The stencil is laid on the surface to be decorated. Dye or paint is wiped over it to reproduce the design through the holes.

Techniques Methods or skills.

Textiles All kinds of fabric, or the threads used to make fabric.

Tjanting A batik tool. Wax is dribbled through a thin nozzle onto the cloth.

Tradition A custom that has been practiced over many years, by one generation of people after another.

FURTHER INFORMATION

BOOKS TO READ

Belfer, Nancy. *Batik and Tie-Dye Techniques*, Third, Rev. Ed. (New York: Dover, 1992).

Kafka, Francis J. *Batik, Tie-Dying, Stenciling, Silk Screen, Block Printing: The Hand Decoration of Fabrics* (New York: Dover, 1973).

Kreider, Kathryn. *Tie-Dye! Easy Instructions for 20 Fantastic Projects.* (Chicago: Contemporary Books, 1989).

Lancaster, John *Fabric Art* (New York: Franklin Watts, 1991)

Readers Digest Crafts & Hobbies (Pleasantville, N.Y. 1979).

SUPPLIERS

Some suppliers of materials for batik and tie-dye are listed below. Also check the Yellow Pages in the telephone directory.

Aljo Manufacturing
  Company
81-83 Franklin Street
New York, NY 10013

Cerulean Blue Ltd
P.O. Box 21168
Seattle, WA 98111

Earth Guild
One Tingle Alley, Dept. T
Asheville, NC 28801

Ruppert, Gibbon & Spider,
  Inc.
718 College Street
Healdburg, CA 95448

For further information about arts and crafts, write to the following organization:

American Craft Council
72 Spring Street
New York, NY 10012

INDEX

ACKNOWLEDGMENTS

The publishers would like to thank the following for allowing their photographs to be reproduced: Bridgeman Art Library 26 right; Bruce Coleman Limited 26 left (G. McCarthy), 27 top left (J. and D. Bartlett); Eye Ubiquitous title page (J. Highet), 4 top (J. Dwyer), 4 bottom (J. Highet), 7 top and bottom right (J. Highet), 7 bottom left (L. Goffin), 12 right, 13 top (P. Seheult), 13 bottom, 27 top center; Hutchison Library 6 right, 12 top left (J. Highet), 12 bottom left (V. and A. Wilkins); Panos Pictures 6 left; Tony Stone Worldwide 27 top and bottom right (L. Burgess); Zefa 27 bottom left, center (G. Kalt). All other photographs, including cover, were supplied by Zul Mukhida. Logo artwork was supplied by John Yates.

The painting *Yellow, Grey, Black* by Jackson Pollock appears by kind permission of the copyright holders: © 1992 The Pollock-Krasner Foundation/ARS N.Y.